The
Oregon Trail

Sabrina Crewe and Michael V. Uschan

Gareth Stevens Publishing

A WORLD ALMANAC EDUCATION GROUP COMPANY

Please visit our web site at: www.garethstevens.com
For a free color catalog describing Gareth Stevens Publishing's list of high-quality
books and multimedia programs, call 1-800-542-2595 (USA) or 1-800-387-3178
(Canada). Gareth Stevens Publishing's fax: (414) 332-3567.

Library of Congress Cataloging-in-Publication Data

Crewe, Sabrina.
     The Oregon Trail / by Sabrina Crewe and Michael V. Uschan.
         p. cm. — (Events that shaped America)
     Includes bibliographical references and index.
     ISBN 0-8368-3405-4 (lib. bdg.)
     1. Oregon National Historic Trail—Juvenile literature. 2. Frontier and pioneer
life—West (U.S.)—Juvenile literature. 3. Overland journeys to the Pacific—Juvenile
literature. 4. West (U.S.)—History—19th century—Juvenile literature. 5. Oregon—
History—To 1859—Juvenile literature. I. Uschan, Michael V., 1948- . II. Title.
III. Series.
     F597.C88   2004
     978'.02—dc22   2004045269

This North American edition first published in 2005 by
Gareth Stevens Publishing
A World Almanac Education Group Company
330 West Olive Street, Suite 100
Milwaukee, WI 53212 USA

This edition © 2005 by Gareth Stevens Publishing.

Produced by Discovery Books
Editor: Sabrina Crewe
Designer and page production: Sabine Beaupré
Photo researcher: Sabrina Crewe
Maps and diagrams: Stefan Chabluk
Gareth Stevens editor: Jim Mezzanotte
Gareth Stevens art direction: Tammy West
Gareth Stevens production: Jessica Morris

Photo credits: Corbis: pp. 6, 9, 10, 11, 12, 14, 15, 20, 23, 24, 25, 26; The Granger
Collection: p. 19; North Wind Picture Archives: cover, pp. 5, 7, 8, 16, 17, 18, 21, 22, 27.

Printed in the United States of America

1 2 3 4 5 6 7 8 9 09 08 07 06 05 04

1031606

Contents

Introduction 4

Chapter 1: Oregon Country 6

Chapter 2: Westward Expansion 12

Chapter 3: On the Oregon Trail 16

Chapter 4: At the End of the Trail 24

Conclusion 26

Time Line 28

Things to Think About and Do 29

Glossary 30

Further Information 31

Index 32

Introduction

This map shows how the United States grew over time. The Oregon Trail helped settlers reach the West.

An Expanding Nation

When the United States was founded in 1776, it consisted of thirteen states in the eastern part of North America. It didn't take long, however, for the new nation to start growing. In 1783, Britain gave the United States an area of land stretching west to the Mississippi River. Then the United States doubled its size with the Louisiana Purchase, a huge region that became a **U.S. territory** in 1803, when it was bought from France. The nation now extended westward from the Mississippi River to the Rocky Mountains.

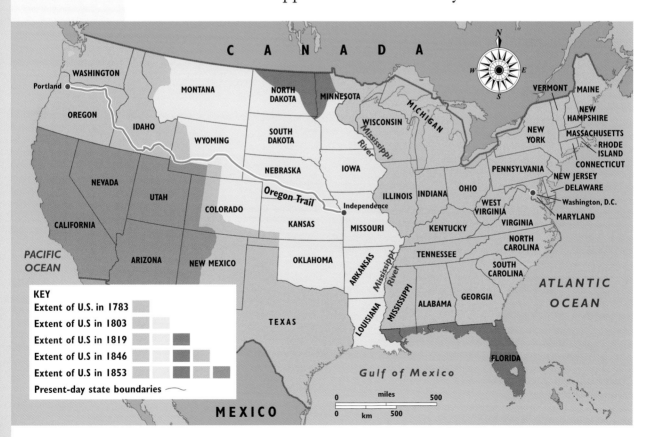

KEY
Extent of U.S. in 1783
Extent of U.S in 1803
Extent of U.S in 1819
Extent of U.S in 1846
Extent of U.S in 1853
Present-day state boundaries

Over the Mountains

What about the land west of the Rockies? In the early 1800s, some of that land was claimed by Mexico, some by the United States, and some by Britain. It took many more years, a number of **treaties**, and even a couple of wars before the United States managed to extend its borders all the way to the Pacific Ocean.

An Important Trail

There was something else—just as important as the treaties and the wars—that helped the nation grow. From the 1840s to the 1860s, the Oregon Trail was the only practical route on which Americans could travel west of the Rocky Mountains. The path began in Missouri and went more than 2,000 miles (3,200 kilometers) across rolling **plains**, high deserts, and snow-capped mountains.

Beginning in the early 1840s, many thousands of people began traveling west along the Oregon Trail. They were settlers, moving to the **West** in search of land and a better life. By wagon, on horseback, and on foot, it was a difficult and dangerous journey that took four to six months. Because of the Oregon Trail, however, white Americans began to settle all over the West.

Thousands of wagons traveled on the Oregon Trail. These ruts along the trail were worn into the rock by the wagons' wheels.

Enduring the Trail

"A man must be able to endure heat like a Salamander, mud and water like a muskrat, dust like a toad, and labor like a jackass. He must learn to eat with his unwashed fingers, sleep on the ground when it rains, and share his blanket with vermin. He must cease to think, except as to where he may find grass and water and a good camping place."

A traveler comments on the hardships of the Oregon Trail, 1852

Chapter One

Oregon Country

A Wonderful Place

The Oregon Trail ended in what was, in the 1800s, called Oregon Country. This huge area in the Pacific Northwest sprawled westward from the Rocky Mountains to the Pacific Ocean and north from California into what is now Canada.

The first white people arriving in Oregon Country found a wonderful place, rich in wildlife, rivers and lakes, and forests. It looked like a good place to settle, and of course it was already settled by many Native American tribes. Oregon Country had been inhabited for more than ten thousand years by the time Europeans came there.

Native Peoples of the Northwest

Some tribes of the Northwest, such as the Chinook, Clatsop, Tillamook, and Tlingit, built their villages along the ocean

The town of Astoria at the mouth of the Columbia River was founded by white settlers in 1811. They used Fort Astoria to trade with the Native people for furs.

The peoples of the Northwest were superb canoe builders and skillful fishers who depended on the ocean and rivers for their food. These people are fishing for salmon on the Columbia River.

shore or on nearby offshore islands. Most of what they ate came from the sea, including whales and seals.

Living in the forests to the east were the Cayuse, Coeur D'Alene, Flathead, Nez Percé, Walla Walla, and Yakama. These tribes lived on salmon and other fish caught in the many rivers that ran through their homelands.

Oregon peoples were hunters as well as fishermen. They caught animals—sea otter, fox, beaver, and others—that they killed for their furs.

The Arrival of Europeans

Furs were prized by white people, too. From the 1500s to the 1800s, people would sail along the Oregon coast to explore and **trade** weapons and other goods for furs. At first, the sailors came from Spain and Britain; later, they came from Russia and the United States.

Staking Claims

On May 11, 1792, Robert Gray, a ship's captain from Boston, sailed his ship, the *Columbia Rediviva*, into the mouth of a large river in Oregon Country. It was called the Oregon River by the people who lived there, but Gray renamed the river "Columbia" after his ship. He also claimed the whole area for the United States.

Just a few months later, in October, Captain George Vancouver also sailed into the Columbia River and claimed the Pacific Northwest for Britain. It was already the homeland of thousands of Native people, but that wasn't even considered. For the next fifty years or so, the United States and Britain would compete to rule the region.

President Jefferson told William Clark and Meriwether Lewis to bring back details of their expedition to the West, including information about wildlife. This page from Clark's records describes a pheasant.

The Mission of Lewis and Clark

"The object of your mission is to explore the Missouri River and such principal streams of it, as, by its course and communication with the waters of the Pacific Ocean, may offer the most direct & practicable [travel route] across this continent for the purposes of commerce."

President Thomas Jefferson's instructions to Lewis and Clark, 1803

Oregon's Destiny

"I am persuaded that Oregon is destined to be the great place of North America. He who can go, and grow with the country, will and must, in three or four years, possess wealth and influence, and greater security, than can be obtained anywhere else."

John Floyd, Virginia congressman, in a letter written March 17, 1824

Lewis and Clark

Before long, white people began coming to Oregon Country overland from the East. The first were the explorers William Clark and Meriwether Lewis, who reached Oregon with the other members of their expedition in 1805.

When he got back to the United States, Clark claimed that the West was "richer in beaver and otter than any country on earth." The promise of riches to be made in the fur trade brought a flood of **trappers** westward to the Rocky Mountains and Oregon Country. By 1824, British and U.S. fur companies were battling for control of Oregon Country.

Every year, a huge *rendezvous* (a French word for "meeting") was held. Mountain men and Native trappers traded with the fur companies, feasted, and competed in games.

Ancient Trails

The fur trappers were an adventurous group known as mountain men. Many became legendary figures of the West. Jedediah Smith, John Colter, James Beckwourth, Jim Bridger, and others pursued their prey all over Oregon Country and the Rocky Mountains. They came across game trails, rivers, lakes, and mountain paths that made their journeys easier. Although they often claimed to be the first to discover these routes, they were in fact journeying along trails used by Native Americans for thousands of years. Over time, the best paths would be woven together into the Oregon Trail.

James Bridger (1804–1881)

James (Jim) Bridger was among the most famous and adventurous of the mountain men. He first went to the West when he took part in an expedition to the Upper Missouri at the age of seventeen. From the 1820s to the 1830s, he worked as a trapper for fur companies, including his own Rocky Mountain Fur Company.

In 1841, Bridger founded a trading post in the southwest corner of present-day Wyoming, on the path to the West that would become the Oregon Trail. Within a short space of time, Fort Bridger was flourishing as an important stopping place for **emigrants**, who would arrive there exhausted and short of supplies.

South Pass got its name because it was south of where Lewis and Clark crossed the Rocky Mountains. It was the best place for wagons to get through the mountains, and it became a vital part of the Oregon Trail.

Finding a Pass

On October 22, 1812, Robert Stuart of the Pacific Fur Company was following a Crow Indian trail through the Rocky Mountains to take supplies west. He found a **pass** so wide and flat that horses and wagons could cross through it. It led over the mountains down to the **Great Plains**. Now known as South Pass, it became a vital part of the route through the Rockies for those traveling the Oregon Trail.

A Way for Wagons

In 1830, Jedediah Smith left St. Louis, Missouri, with ten wagons loaded with supplies for trappers in the West. He led the wagons over South Pass, the first time wagons had traveled all the way west over the Rocky Mountains. Smith proved that settlers and their families could make the journey with wagons to carry supplies and personal possessions.

Chapter Two

Westward Expansion

This print illustrates the idea of Manifest Destiny. It shows white civilization—in the form of houses, trains, and wagons—spreading westward while the Native people move aside.

Powerful Forces

In the 1840s, two powerful forces began to motivate people in the United States. "**Manifest** Destiny" was the term used to describe the belief that God had given white, Christian Americans the right to control all of the North American continent. "Oregon Fever" was the name given to the desire that many possessed to move west along the Oregon Trail.

Manifest Destiny

Back in 1818, the United States and Britain had agreed to joint ownership of Oregon Country. But in 1845, President James K. Polk claimed, "Our title to the country of the Oregon is clear and unquestionable." He was a passionate believer in Manifest Destiny and **westward expansion**.

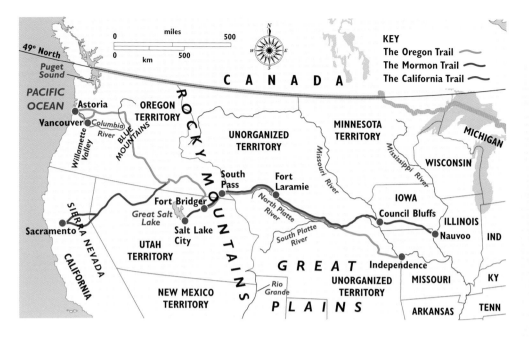

This map shows the West in 1848. It also shows the **Mormon** and California Trails that split off from the Oregon Trail to take people to other parts of the West.

In 1846, after much argument, the two countries agreed to a boundary through Oregon Country, dividing it between the United States and Canada, then a British territory. That line is now the border between the state of Washington and the Canadian province of British Columbia.

Within a couple of years, Polk had also fought for and won the Mexican territories of California and the Southwest. By 1848, U.S. territory stretched to the Pacific Ocean, and Manifest Destiny had become a reality.

Oregon Fever

At the same time, the Oregon Trail was starting to get busy. Oregon Fever was caused by several things. Farmers in the East were having a tough time getting by, and land was expensive. Life in the crowded, dirty cities of the East was difficult. By going west, people could acquire cheap, free land in a place with a good climate and rich soil. Glowing reports were coming back from **pioneers** who had already moved to Oregon, such as the **missionary** Marcus Whitman.

The Fever Rages

"The Oregon Fever is raging in almost every part of the Union. . . . It would be reasonable to suppose that there will be at least five thousand [more] Americans west of the Rocky Mountains by next autumn."

The Iowa Gazette *newspaper, 1840*

Missionaries Head West

The first people to travel the Oregon Trail after the traders and fur trappers were missionaries, who went west to convert American Indians to Christianity. In 1834, Methodist Reverend Jason Lee built a **mission** on the Willamette River in Oregon. Two missionary couples—Marcus and Narcissa Whitman and Henry and Eliza Spalding—then set out from western New York in 1836. Whitman and Spalding were the first white women to travel the Oregon Trail.

The fact that they survived the rugged journey in a wagon was proof that families could use this new route to move west. Although the trip was rough, Narcissa Whitman loved it. "I never was so contented and happy before, neither have I enjoyed such health for years," she wrote in a daily journal that has become one of the classic accounts of life on the Oregon Trail.

The Pend D'Oreille mission in the Rocky Mountains.

Just a few hundred emigrants went west in 1841 and 1842. The trickle of newcomers along the Oregon Trail grew to a flood in 1843, however, when 1,000 people made the trek. In 1844, another 1,400 people headed west, and this number was more than doubled in 1845 when 3,000 emigrants traveled the Oregon Trail. The movement became known as "the Great **Migration**."

There are no records to show how many people migrated. Historians guess that between 250,000 and 650,000 people had traveled along the Oregon Trail by the end of the 1860s.

Different Routes and Names

Before becoming known as the Oregon Trail, the route had other names. Originally, it was called simply the "trapper's route." In the early 1840s, when American settlers started using the path to head west, it became known first as the Emigrant Road. After 1845, it was also referred to as the Oregon and California Trail, and eventually it became known as just the Oregon Trail.

Thousands of emigrants etched their names in Independence Rock, a landmark along the trail in central Wyoming.

Chapter Three

On the Oregon Trail

Wagon Trains

The journey west along the Oregon Trail took between four and six months. The trail began on the outskirts of Independence, Missouri. Every spring, emigrants gathered in Missouri to form groups called wagon trains. These teams would make the journey together and could number from a few dozen wagons to hundreds. It was safest to travel in wagon trains when things got difficult because people could help each other. Most emigrants chose oxen to pull their wagons. Oxen were slower than horses and mules, but they were strong and dependable.

The wagons that traveled the Oregon Trail were nicknamed "prairie schooners." Their high, rounded white tops reminded people of a type of ship called a schooner, which had a large white sail.

A large wagon train makes its camp on the Plains before heading into the mountains.

Wagon trains were usually guided by former mountain men. There were other leaders as well: a captain and officers to make daily decisions, such as where to camp each night. Groups discussed and agreed upon general rules about behavior and safety for the journey ahead.

Supplies for the Journey

Travelers filled their wagons with basic supplies—food, clothing, cooking pots, tools, medicine, spare parts for wagons, and personal belongings. To reach the Pacific Northwest, a family of four needed 1,000 pounds (450 kilograms) of food, including some 150 pounds (70 kg) of bacon and 200 pounds (90 kg) of flour. Most families started with a few cattle and some chickens and pigs, all of which could be eaten on the way. Every family had at least one gun for protection and for hunting buffalo and other animals for meat.

Daily Life on the Trail

A day on the trail started before dawn, around 4:00 A.M. Travelers made a fire to cook breakfast. They often used dried buffalo droppings because wood was scarce. They usually ate sowbelly and slam-johns (their names for bacon and pancakes), a meal they might have day after day. Emigrant Helen Carpenter once joked that "about the only change [in diet] we have from bread and bacon, is bacon and bread." When meat ran out, people killed buffalo for food along the way.

As the sun rose, people hitched oxen to their wagons and began moving west in a long line. Almost everyone walked because the wagons were so heavily loaded. They would stop around noon for lunch and then continue on until dark. Then the travelers would form a protective circle with their wagons and set up camp.

Travelers made slow progress on the Oregon Trail with all their animals and possessions. They usually traveled between 10 and 20 miles (16 and 32 km) in a day.

Buffalo Meat

"Not one in our number relishes buffalo meat as well as my husband and I. He has a different way for cooking every piece of meat. We have meat and tea in the morn, and tea and meat at noon. . . . I relish it well and it agrees with me. My health is excellent. I never saw any thing like buffalo meat to satisfy hunger."

Narcissa Whitman, journal entry on the Oregon Trail, 1836

No Water, No Grass

"The last of the Black Hills we crossed this afternoon. . . .
Not a drop of water, nor a spear of grass to be seen, nothing
but barren hills, bare broken rock, sand and dust. We reached
Platte River about noon, and our cattle were so crazy for
water that some of them plunged head long into the river.
Traveled 18 miles [29 km] and camp[ed]."

Emigrant Amelia Stewart Knight, journal entry, July 11, 1853

Crossing Rivers

The journey began easily enough across the flat Great Plains.
Even on the Plains, however, it was difficult to cross rivers.
The emigrants usually floated their wagons across, with
people and animals having to swim. In shallow water, wagon
trains sometimes became stuck in mud.

A group of Sioux sit nearby as emigrants cross the Platte River. Many lives and belongings were lost in the rivers along the Oregon Trail.

People who traveled the Oregon Trail were not just going to Oregon Country. Everyone began their trip on the trail because it was the only route over the Rocky Mountains. Two other trails, however, branched off from the Oregon Trail after it crossed that range (see the map on page 13). The Mormon Trail split off to the south after Fort Bridger, in what is now Wyoming. From 1846, thousands of Mormons used the Oregon and Mormon Trails to reach their new homes in Utah. Settlers who wanted to go to California left the Oregon Trail in Idaho and began journeying southwest along the California Trail to reach their destination. The Oregon and California Trails became heavily traveled by gold seekers when the California Gold Rush started in 1849.

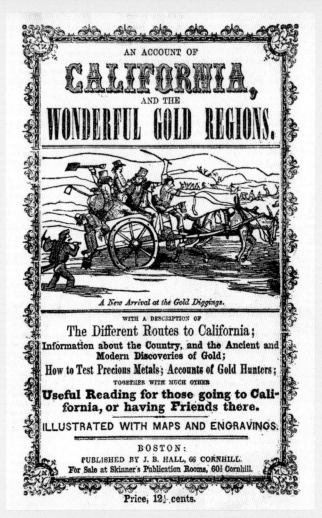

AN ACCOUNT OF

CALIFORNIA,

AND THE

WONDERFUL GOLD REGIONS.

A New Arrival at the Gold Diggings.

WITH A DESCRIPTION OF

The Different Routes to California;

Information about the Country, and the Ancient and Modern Discoveries of Gold;

How to Test Precious Metals; Accounts of Gold Hunters;

TOGETHER WITH MUCH OTHER

Useful Reading for those going to California, or having Friends there.

ILLUSTRATED WITH MAPS AND ENGRAVINGS.

BOSTON:
PUBLISHED BY J. B. HALL, 66 CORNHILL.
For Sale at Skinner's Publication Rooms, 60½ Cornhill.

Price, 12½ cents.

A brochure encourages people to emigrate along the Oregon and California Trails during the Gold Rush.

Getting through the Mountains

The trail became harder as it entered the Rocky Mountains. And after the Rockies, travelers on the California Trail had to get through the Sierra Nevada, and those bound for Oregon Country had to pass over the Blue Mountains.

A man pushes from behind as oxen strain to pull a wagon up the steep mountain path. By the trail is the skeleton of an ox that didn't make it over the mountains.

It was backbreaking work to get wagons through the mountains. On the steepest parts of the trail, travelers would combine many animals into one team to pull the wagons, one by one, up the mountain paths. The animals would then come back down, and the exhausting process would be repeated for each wagon. People often had to lighten their wagons by throwing things out, including treasured possessions.

The Mormons

Mormons began traveling the Oregon and Mormon Trails in 1846. Those who were too poor to buy wagons pushed their belongings west in handcarts. Thousands of Mormons trekked to Utah in this way. In 1856, three of five groups of Mormons pushing handcarts made it through, but two others started late and encountered bad winter weather. More than two hundred people died from cold and starvation.

Death on the Trail

Altogether, probably more than 34,000 people died on the Oregon Trail. They died from thirst, starvation, accidents, and attacks by Indians or robbers. Bad weather killed numbers of people: There were lightning strikes, fierce storms that produced flash floods, and **drought** conditions. Hundreds of people drowned in the Platte, Kansas, and Columbia Rivers.

The major cause of death was illness, especially cholera, the single largest killer on the Oregon Trail. There was no

This group of Mormons, many on foot and pushing handcarts, struggled through terrible weather to reach the Mormon capital of Salt Lake City. Many of them died on the way.

The Mormon Handcart Song
"Some must push and some must pull, As we go marching up the hill, So merrily on our way we go Until we reach the valley, O!"

Lyrics to a Mormon song

This busy scene at Fort Laramie, painted by Alfred Jacob Miller, shows Native Americans at the outpost when it was a fur-trading center. Fort Laramie later served many emigrants with supplies and a place to rest on the Oregon Trail.

cure for cholera, which swept in **epidemics** through entire wagon trains. The disease produced high fevers and vomiting and could kill a person in less than a day.

Native Americans

The Oregon Trail sliced through the ancient homelands of many peoples before it reached the Native territories of Oregon Country. The Pawnee, Sioux, and Cheyenne lived on the Great Plains. The Arapaho, Blackfeet, and Shoshone lived in the Rocky Mountains. The California and Mormon Trails also went through land inhabited by many tribes.

Most encounters between emigrants and Native Americans were friendly. When the two groups met on the trail, they often traded for things needed by both sides, with emigrants offering clothes, tobacco, and iron tools in exchange for food or horses.

Over time, as the number of travelers increased, Indians began to resent whites trekking across their lands. Some groups of Indians stole horses and cattle. Attacks on wagon trains, however, were rare. Historians guess that, between 1840 and 1860, about 360 emigrants were killed by Indians, while more than 400 Indians were killed by whites.

Chapter Four

At the End of the Trail

A photograph, taken in Washington about 1890, shows a typical homestead for emigrants arriving in the Northwest.

Building a New Home

"Father built his first cabin on . . . a ridge . . . above the valley. In the course of three or four years . . . we had pastures fenced, grain fields and gardens, small apple and peach orchards, comfortable log cabins, barns, and other outhouses, and quite a number of cattle, horses, hogs, and chicken."

Oregon settler Jesse Applegate describing his family's settlement, 1843

Hard Work

The end of the trip west meant the beginning of years of hard work. Most people started from scratch. They had to build their own homes and clear away trees and brush before planting corn, wheat, and other basic food crops. Settlers who came in later years could buy farms that already had cultivated fields and a house.

Taking Land and Bringing Disease

The white invasion was a disaster for the people of Oregon Country. Emigrants seized land and disrupted hunting and fishing. The newcomers also introduced diseases, such as measles, chicken pox, and cholera, that killed many thousands of Native people.

Many Cayuse people of Oregon ended up on the Umatilla Reservation. This picture, taken on the reservation by Edward Curtis in 1910, is of a Cayuse woman in ceremonial dress.

Conflicts between whites and Indians raged until the 1870s, when the U.S. military wiped out the last Native resistance in Oregon. In 1877, the U.S. Army ordered Chief Joseph of the Nez Percé and eight hundred of his people to a **reservation** in what is now Idaho. When the Indians tried to escape to Canada, the army chased and fought them across 2,000 miles (3,200 km) of Oregon Country. Chief Joseph surrendered on October 5, 1877, in present-day Montana.

The Cayuse and the Whitmans

Narcissa and Marcus Whitman, who had arrived in 1836, built their mission at Wailatpu. In 1846, Cayuse children at the mission school caught measles, starting an epidemic that swept through their tribe. The Whitmans tried and failed to save the sick, and Indian leaders blamed the couple for the deaths. On November 29, Chief Tilokaikt led a party that killed a dozen people, including the Whitmans, and kidnapped fifty white men, women, and children. The killings started the Cayuse War, in which the Cayuse were hunted down and killed or placed on reservations.

Conclusion

The rounded shape of Independence Rock rises above the Sweetwater River in central Wyoming. Carved in its sides are thousands of names, each with its own story to tell.

Independence Rock

On July 4, 1824, trappers led by Thomas Fitzpatrick camped by a large granite rock rising out of the Great Plains in what is now Wyoming. They named it Independence Rock in honor of the national holiday that day. It became known as the "Great Register of the Desert" because emigrants etched their names on it. Clearly visible from a distance, the rock became a welcome milestone for emigrants. Today, it is still a reminder of those who traveled the Oregon Trail.

We Go Westward

"Eastward I go only by force, but westward I go free. This is the prevailing tendency of my countrymen. I must walk toward Oregon. We go westward as into the future, with a spirit of enterprise and adventure."

Henry David Thoreau, "Walking," Atlantic Monthly magazine, June 1862

End of the Oregon Trail

On May 10, 1869, the Union Pacific and Central Pacific Railroads met at Promontory Summit, Utah, to connect the nation's first railroad across the West. After that, most people heading west traveled on the Transcontinental Railroad. By the 1870s, the Oregon Trail was no longer needed.

Creating New States

The many thousands who had traveled the Oregon Trail, however, had made a huge impact. They did not just make new homes for themselves, but helped create new states.

The right to acquire statehood depended on population. Because of the Gold Rush, California's population boomed, and it become the nation's thirty-first state on September 9, 1850. That year, Oregon still had fewer than twelve thousand white settlers, and the territory did not become a state until February 14, 1859.

Settlement was slower in other areas reached by Oregon Trail emigrants. But the people who migrated west along the trail set a pattern that later created the states of Washington and Montana (both 1889), Idaho and Wyoming (both 1890), and Utah (1896).

Towns sprang up and territories became states as more and more emigrants arrived in the West. This is the main street of Walla Walla in Washington in the 1890s.

1783	Britain grants territory east of Mississippi River to the United States.
1792	May 11: Captain Robert Gray claims Pacific Northwest for the United States.
	October: Captain George Vancouver claims Pacific Northwest for Britain.
1803	Louisiana Purchase.
1805	Lewis and Clark expedition reaches Oregon.
1812	October 22: Robert Stuart travels over and names South Pass.
1818	October 20: United States and Britain sign Oregon Joint Occupation Treaty.
1824	July 4: Trappers camp by and name Independence Rock in present-day Wyoming.
1830	Jedediah Smith leads first wagon train over Rocky Mountains.
1834	Reverend Jason Lee founds mission in Willamette Valley.
1836	Whitmans and Spaldings travel to Willamette Valley along Oregon Trail.
1841–42	A few hundred emigrants travel west on Oregon Trail.
1843	1,000 emigrants travel west on Oregon Trail.
1844	1,400 emigrants travel west on Oregon Trail.
1845	3,000 emigrants travel west on Oregon Trail.
1846	June 18: United States and Britain agree on U.S.-Canadian border.
	Whitmans are killed by Cayuse Indians, sparking Cayuse War.
	First Mormons travel along Oregon and Mormon Trails to Utah.
1848	January: Gold discovery in California causes Gold Rush to begin in 1849.
1850	California becomes a state.
1859	Oregon becomes a state.
1869	May 10: Transcontinental Railroad is completed.
1877	Nez Percé are defeated by U.S. Army.
1889	Washington and Montana become states.
1890	Idaho and Wyoming becomes states.
1896	Utah becomes a state.

Things to Think About and Do

Native Americans in the Northwest

Find out more about the Native American tribes that lived in the Northwest. Write about the impact on their lives of the first white explorers, the mountain men, and finally the emigrants who came along the Oregon Trail to settle in the West.

Along the Trail

Imagine you and your family have traveled west along the Oregon Trail in the 1850s. Write about your experience along the trail and afterward, when you arrived and settled in Oregon, California, or Utah.

Glossary

drought: period of low rainfall that causes shortages of water.

emigrant: person who leaves his or her country of residence and goes to live somewhere else.

epidemic: rapid spread of disease that affects a large number of people.

Great Plains: area of North America between the Mississippi River and the Rocky Mountains.

manifest: obviously true and easily recognizable. White Americans in the mid-1800s believed it was obviously their destiny to take over the North American continent.

migration: movement from one place to another.

mission: center built to convert Native Americans to Christianity.

missionary: person who believes it is his or her duty to convert other people to his or her own religion.

Mormon: member of the Church of Jesus Christ of the Latter Day Saints.

pass: low place in a mountain range that allows access to the other side.

pioneer: person who does something first, such as settle in new territory.

plains: large areas of flat or rolling land without trees.

reservation: public land set aside for Native American people to live on when they were removed from their homelands.

trade: exchange one thing for another using goods instead of money.

trapper: hunter who uses traps to kill animals for fur.

treaty: agreement made among two or more people or groups of people after negotiations.

U.S. territory: geographical area that belongs to and is governed by the United States but is not included in any of its states.

West: term used in the 1800s for area of North America west of the United States.

westward expansion: process of growth of the United States in the 1800s.

Further Information

Books
Blackwood, Gary L. *Life on the Oregon Trail* (The Way People Live). Lucent, 1999.

Kimball, Violet T. *Stories of Young Pioneers: In Their Own Words*. Mountain Press, 2000.

Moeller, Bill and Jan Moeller. *The Oregon Trail: A Photographic Journey*. Mountain Press, 2003.

Web Sites
www.bluebook.state.or.us State of Oregon web site has a wealth of information on the Oregon Trail and how it helped Oregon grow.

www.endoftheoregontrail.org National Oregon Trail Interpretive Center has information and pictures, including a section on African-American settlers.

www.nps.gov/fola Fort Laramie National Historic Site web site offers information about Fort Laramie's history and about the site today.

Useful Addresses
The National Oregon Trail Interpretive Center
P.O. Box 987
Baker City, OR 97814
Telephone: (503) 523-1845

National Park Service
Long Distance Trails Office
324 South State Street, Suite 250
P.O. Box 45155
Salt Lake City, UT 84145-0155
Telephone: (801) 539-4095

Index

Page numbers in **bold** indicate pictures.

Astoria, **6**, **13**

Blue Mountains, **13**, 20
Bridger, James, 10, **10**
Britain, 4, 5, 7, 8, 9, 12

California, 6, 13, **13**, 20, **20**, 27
California Trail, **13**, 15, 20, **20**, 23
Canada, 6, 13, **13**, 25
Chief Joseph, 25
Columbia River, **7**, 8, **13**, 22

emigrants, 5, 10, 14, 16, 17, **17**, **18**, **20**, **21**, **22**, 26
    experiences of, 16, 18, 19, 20, 21, 22, 23, 24
    numbers of, 5, 15, 22

Fort Bridger, 10, **13**, 20
Fort Laramie, **13**, **23**
fur traders and trappers, 7, 9, **9**, 10, **10**, 11, 14, 26

Great Plains, 11, **13**, **17**, 19

Independence, **4**, **13**, 16
Independence Rock, **15**, 26, **26**

Jefferson, Thomas, 8

Lewis and Clark expedition, 8, **8**, 9, 11

Manifest Destiny, 12, **12**, 13
missions and missionaries, 13, 14, **14**
Mormon Trail, **13**, 20, 22, **22**, 23
Mormons, 20, 22, **22**
mountain men, **9**, 10, **10**, 17

Native Americans, 6, 7, **7**, 8, **9**, 10, 11, **12**, **19**, 22, 23, **23**, 24, 25, **25**

Oregon (state), 27
Oregon Country, 6, 7, 8, 9, 10, 12, 13, **13**, 20, 23, 24, 25
Oregon Fever, 12, 13
Oregon Trail, **4**, 5, **5**, 6, 10, 11, 13, **13**, 15, 20, 27
    traveling on, 14, 15, 16–23, **17**, **18**, **19**, **21**, 22, 23, 26

Pacific Ocean, **4**, 5, 6, 7, 13, **13**
Polk, James K., 12, 13
prairie schooners, *see* wagons

reservations, 25, **25**
Rocky Mountains, 4, 5, 6, 9, 10, 11, **11**, 13, **13**, 20, 23

Salt Lake City, **13**, 22
settlement and settlers, 5, 11, 15, 24, 25, 27
Sierra Nevada, **13**, 20
Smith, Jedediah, 10, 11
South Pass, 11, **11**, **13**
Spalding, Henry and Eliza, 14

trading posts, 10, **23**
Transcontinental Railroad, 27

United States, 4, **4**, 5, 7, 8, 9, 12
United States territories, 4, 13, **13**, 27
Utah, **13**, 20, 22, 27

wagons and wagon trains, 5, 11, **12**, 14, 16, **16**, 17, **17**, 18, **18**, 19, **19**, **20**, 21, **21**, 22, **22**, 23
Washington, 13, **24**, 27, **27**
West, the, 4, 5, 9, 10, 11, 13, **13**, 27
westward expansion, 4, **4**, 5, 12, 13, 27
Whitman, Marcus and Narcissa, 13, 14, 18, 25
Willamette River and Valley, **13**, 14
Wyoming, 10, **15**, 20, 26, 27